THE INNER ME

LOOKING BACK AT ME

A NOVEL

DR. NATHALIE CHASE THOMPSON

The Inner Me
Looking back at me

Copyright © 2020 Dr. Nathalie Chase Thompson

Cover Design: C Marcel Wiggins
Layout Design: Roy Etienne Smith

Dekan Press by MIGMIR All rights reserved. No part of this publication may be reproduced, distributed or transmitted in any form or by any means, without prior written permission. Unless otherwise identified, scripture quotations are from the King James Version of the Bible.

Published by
MIGMIR Company USA, LLC
P.O. BOX 291354
Port Orange, FL 32129

www.migmir.us

For Worldwide Distribution
Printed in the U.S.A.

ISBN:978-1-952253-07-2

Library of Congress Control Number: 2020946882

CONTENTS

Acknowledgments (4)
Foreword (7)
Introduction (9)

- Chapter **One** -
Open your mouth (13)

- Chapter **Two** -
When will you learn? (21)

- Chapter **Three** -
Trials beginning to pay off (27)

- Chapter **Four** -
When Holy Spirit ministers to you (37)

- Chapter **Five** -
Trusting in your "why" trade off (45)

- Chapter **Six** -
Some things you shouldn't forget (51)

- Chapter **Seven** -
Looking within (57)

- Chapter **Eight** -
Scheduling God (63)

- Chapter **Nine** -
Soundproofing (69)

- Chapter **Ten** -
Purpose in the earth (77)

Journal **Section** (81)

ACKNOWLEDGMENTS

To my children, Balaam Fields, Sr. and Natasha Fields, our lives have been like reading a book, but we made it. Thank you for loving me when at times I didn't deserve it. My prayer will always be that The Hand of God continuously be upon you to guide and protect you and my grands. I love you to Life.

To Apostle Roy and Dr. EShawnna Smith, short and simple, thank you for standing with me and pushing me.

To Apostle Ron Toliver, "Holy Spirit Divine connection." I came aboard the KRGA cruise, November 2018, simply for Holy Spirit to reveal that He'd connected us 4 years prior. Thank you for activation and PUSHING!

To Apostle Monique Harris, oh how I love you. My life has been changed for the better ever since you became a part of it.

To Apostle A.T. Jones Sr. and Bishop Sharon Jones, thankful we all realized the why. The love and admiration I have for you both will never change. Throughout the pages of my life you will be found.

To my friend Pastor Mary Jo Jackson, thank you for always "keeping it real" as you say. I would not have it any other way.

To Pastors Willie James & Mary Stewart BOOM! That's how we came together. Yes, we will remain. Sis, you are my confidant and shoulder.

To Pastors Mike Ragan and Dee Ragan Sr., your prayers, wisdom, and teachings have grounded me during this time of my life. Continue doing what you do. There are many sons and daughters yet to come.

My Call to Apostleship 2016 Accepted

This was not the life I chose for myself but chosen for me. Over the years, I have come to embrace this new life I now live with a purpose. I realize God chose me to aid in the building of HIS Kingdom is both a privilege and an honor. I do not see myself as being "the one" who made it all come together, but being a servant following the instructions of THE ONE who created all.

We all have life lessons and what we walk away with will determine our destiny. From my childhood to this day, I have always been a cheerleader for the underdog. Now from the naked eye, you may never be able to recognize who these people are. Some of them are CEO's, ministry leaders, husbands, wives, homeless, and educated—young and old alike.

Someone once asked me, "What confirmed in me that my call to ministry was from God?" My answer was and still is, "Over these 57 years the life I've lived." As you continue to read, you will better understand this statement. This is in no way to appear arrogant but if it had not been for The Lord who was on my side, Nathalie would not be here today.

Everyone has a story to tell but there is only one you. Not the you who you present to people, but the you who cannot hide the hurt, fear, loneliness, or anguish. The you who wants to give up but cannot. The you who wants to walk away but will not. The you who knows there are so many who do not have a voice, no direction, and no protection. The you who fell. The you who was put out and put down by people in church, family members, and society alike. I am still here. I know my call is an election sure.

As recorded in Jeremiah 1:4-10(CJB)

Here is the word of Adonai that came to me: "Before I formed you in the womb, I knew you; before you were born, I separated you for myself. I have appointed you to be a prophet to the nations." I said, "Oh, Adonai Elohim, I don't even know how to speak! I'm just a child!" But Adonai said to me, "Don't say, 'I'm just a child, "For you will go to whomever I send you, and you will speak whatever I order you. Do not be afraid of them, for I am with you, says Adonai, to rescue you." Then Adonai put out his hand and touched my mouth, and Adonai said to me "There! I have put my words in your mouth. Today I have placed you over nations and kingdoms to uproot and to tear down, to destroy and to demolish, to build and to plant."

I will always remember that everything I do is not done of my own doing, but by divine ordinance of God HIMSELF. To maintain a servant's heart is imperative. My prayer is to always remain humble no matter where He takes me, who He places me before, or what He allows me to obtain. Teaching others the Word walk of Christ is a lifestyle, not a job. My joy comes from seeing others obtain victory and walk into their destinies. By doing so, the scripture will be manifested as in Matthew 25:31-46 "... for when I was hungry, I was thirsty, I was a stranger, Naked, I was sick, I was in prison, and you came to me....Then shall HE answer them, saying, Verily I say unto you, inasmuch as ye have done it unto one of the least of these my brethren, ye have done it unto me." I am committed to teach and live these principles out through each lane of God's "LifesReDesign" of Nathalie's life in Christ.

Apostle Nathalie Chase Thompson

FOREWORD

The body of Christ welcomes a fresh heart and new approach to helping us live and go through the many challenges, tumultuous, heart-breaking and disappointing times we face through this journey of life.

We all have experienced one time or the other, hurts, pains and disappointments, that if we only had one person who has gone through the same things and have come out all right, we would know and understand that the same could happen for us. We would have the strength to hold on.

This book has been fashioned and designed to minister from a place of experience. To talk about something and to experience something is very different.

To see someone who heard the call of God for her life, and continued to move forward in spite of all of the opposition, and move forward with a humble heart and submissive spirit, is very encouraging.

As you read this author's personal testimony know this, that the same God that did it for her can do it for you. I have watched her grow even with voices in her ears telling her she cannot do it. Yet she evolved to this place.

I have seen and heard the times that she wanted to give up but knew that she could not. She did not understand the "WHY." But this book has revealed her purpose and the plan mandated by God.

Her transparency and realness is very rewarding in a time when so much is covered up and not revealed because of pride and the way you are viewed before society.

Read this book with anticipation, knowing that the

INNER ME IS LOOKING BACK AT ME will come forth soaring as an eagle flying high into the greater and the better for your life.

Bishop Sharon P. Jones,

All People International Church, Inc.

She Leads Ministry, Jacksonville, Florida

INTRODUCTION

June 8, 2018 @ 12:41a.m. Reflections

I have been blessed to counsel, mentor, and develop several programs that serve families, youth, adults and the incarcerated. During my 30 plus years in the ministry, I founded LifeReDesign Ministry, OpFaith, and Habakkuk 2 School of Ministry. Additionally, the title "author" was added to the line-up of manifestations God has afforded me to experience through His redesign of my life. With all of this, it means nothing if we cannot assist in bringing forth change in the life of another. We should always remember from whence we came. Whatsoever seed we sow in our today, a greater harvest shall we reap in our tomorrows.

Today, transparency is frowned upon by many. They prefer to see you in a position of flawlessness, all the while with hidden terrors. Some of which stems from low self-esteem, insecurity, trust issues, hate, rage, vanity, pride, I can go on and on. When you saw the title, your subconscious automatically stated: "I already know myself." Do you?

Based on our upbringings and culture, our mindsets become molded and formulated. We are taught, what are to be our strengths and weaknesses, true or not. Our environment, as children, created a picture of acceptable living. Adults and those older created visual snapshots and videos of acceptable behavior. Given all the pieces the process begins.

The burden then becomes ours as young children to process it all. Our acting out is looked at as being "cute and funny." If talking back as little children, "oh he/she acts just like you did lol." And it is acceptable—or those that are quiet, polite, and respectful, are placed upon a pedestal and spoiled to be admired. Then you have those that are abused physically, sexually, mentally, and verbally. They create a world within a world. Only a small percentage grow in a "true reality."

Now into our teenage years. What options must we select from? Grown and sassy(girls), grown and smooth(guys). Perhaps still quiet, educated, polite, and respectful. Remember those being abused their world intensifies. Those in the now continue. Decisions for tomorrow are ever-present before us. The time is getting closer every day.

Finally, we are adults on our own and we have our future ahead of us. Decisions, challenges, relationships, careers, families, lifestyle, etc... We have the toolbox of our youth to guide us. Our toolbox has everything that we need for our journey. The blueprint has been drawn out. We are ready. Are you really?

Keep in mind throughout the book your Inner Me will come from one if not each age grouping. Are you or have you truly met yourself face-2-face?

God Answers the Prophet

I will stand at my guard post

And station myself on the tower; And I will keep watch to see what He will say to me,

And what answer I will give [as His spokesman] when I am reproved.

Then the LORD answered me and said, "Write the vision

And engrave it plainly on [clay] tablets, So that the

one who reads it will run.

For the vision is yet for the appointed [future] time…It hurries toward the goal [of fulfillment]; it will not fail. Even though it delays, wait [patiently] for it, Because it will certainly come; it will not delay. Habakkuk 2:1-3 (AMP)

CHAPTER 1
OPEN YOUR MOUTH

This chapter's focus is to empower you to take authority over the voices that have dominated your life's structure. Those that we have allowed to dictate what was correct for us. Dictators of how to dress, think and go, even when God Himself has given us instructions.

Those that have as Eli didn't catch it at first that God was calling you. Once realized,

THE INNER ME

releasing you to go as God has called you, but not before they've permitted you still. Restoring, develop, and shaping the sound of your voice.

I am who YOU (Elohim) say I am and no longer make apologies for being my authentic self. For far too long, I have given voice to others to define "me." As I'm sure so many that are reading this have also. It is called transference of power as well, a spirit of manipulation in action (influencing or attempting to change the behavior or emotions of others for one's own purpose).

We have allowed (past tense, I speak this in Holy Spirit that it is broken NOW in Jesus Name) others to dictate our what/why/when. The ONLY person that should ever have that power is The Father. Funny, HE doesn't take it, for we have FREE WILL. Now understand this comes from childhood to adults, work, ministry, relationships, etc... At some point, you WILL say enough is enough!!!

For you fashioned my inmost being, you knit me together in my mother's womb. I thank you because I am awesomely made, wonderfully; your works are wonders I know this very well. Psalms 139:13,14 (CJB)

Do you see/hear the word says "I Know" once you know something, you can no longer not know it? Even after two strokes, I don't remember everything. What I have found out,

CHAPTER ONE

the right word, event, or emotion comes up; (at times) it triggers me to remember. Opening your mouth is like an outward conscience voice. When you say a thing, you will hear and believe what you hear. Your words shall resurrect power that has been dormant within.

Within the process of planting new grass first, the ground needs to be tilled. Once you turn over the soil, loosen it up, get the weeds out, etc., new life can begin. The same pertains to you and me opening our mouths. At first, I felt that I was selfish. Well, I soon realized that it was a good thing. Not being narcissistic in the sense of disrespect, but of empowering myself. And in the Spirit, I was being liberated from the inside out.

When you have reached that breaking point, good/bad/indifferent, choices and actions are ALWAYS required. I have not always made the best choices, for some were based upon emotions and the heart. Those choices may have devastating consequences attached. Nevertheless, I am blessed to be in a relationship with my Champion Jesus.

Being in a relationship with HIM (Jesus) although trials and tribulations come, and I feel the sting and pain, when in fact it is ALL good. Our part is to learn from our experiences and pay them forward. In doing so when the time is right, that person will either avoid some pitfalls or fall on their faces. Either way, it is a learning process, that is needful. It's NOT up to

THE INNER ME

us to decide.
It is their decision if they take the advice.

Through this part of my life, rejection became a natural, recurring event through times of deep depression and yet ministering to others. I amazed even myself how I could separate the two. When it came to the things of God, I did not matter. Once the assignment was done the anointing lifted and the depression, loneliness—whatever was starring me in my face again.

Depression was a constant companion in my late 20's and early 30's. Lord, the suicide attempts were unreal. I would become so angry with God for not allowing me to die. Just let all this be over Lord, then screaming WHY!! Finally, realizing my flesh was being crucified so that this scripture would come alive within me.

We have all kinds of troubles, but not crushed; we are perplexed, yet not in despair; persecuted, yet not abandoned; knocked down, yet not destroyed..." For we who are alive are always being handed over to death for Yeshua's sake so that Yeshua's life also might be manifested in our mortal bodies.
2 Corinthians 4:8-11 (CJB)

Some will never fit in. I was one of the "some." Be cool with that. It is how The Architect designed you. It is a blessing #squarepeginaroundwhole #youareunique.

CHAPTER ONE

For years I thought there was something wrong with me. I would look in the mirror, and see I was not shaped like others. I did not talk like others, or see things like most.

Lord, what in the Hell is going on?

Yes, I said it!

Why am I always the cast-away?

In a crowded room but all alone. Invited to be on the program, but sitting by myself, traveling with a group but still by myself.

I am a people person, so what am I doing wrong?

For as long as I can remember and even now, I do not fit in. Yes, I have "friends," but we respect each other's lane.

Jesus, I would like to go to the movies, Jazz night, take a trip and do "girl things." When I was a little girl, I would hear myself say," Your life is one that will be lonely and traveled alone." I never liked or understood this until much later in life, and still at times it gets to me. But you know the song, "I got a testimony?" Mine consists of The Lord has been good to me because The Father knew best.

THE INNER ME

Had I been able to hang out as a youth, young adult and even now in my fifties, I wouldn't be writing this now. So many in/out of the church are dead and gone. A large number of them were drug related. As I stated in "And Now I Live," anything that affected my sex life, Nathalie did not want it. The men, if you were unable to satisfy my sexual appetite, you would be cut. FOOLISH me! The inner me did not see me at that time at all.

One of my mentors, the late Elder Jessie Mae Lester, would say to me, "Natlee it's a piss po hoe that gets laid and gets a wet tail. Child, every man that smiles at you and says nice words don't mean you good. WAKE UP!" I have always had my coke shape with that 36" bust 23"-26" waist and 37"-38" hips and worked out and was thick.

I was fornicating because I was a sex addict. Unfortunately, I was not aware of the addiction at the time. And it would rear its ugly head in and through some I never would expect. Lord, I dealt with this when I was younger, why is it that I cannot get away from this? I attracted senior church leaders, police officers, lawyers, business owners and more. Yet, I was just a piece of meat—a trophy to take out when needed. I was a sperm dump, then put back on the shelf (until next time). Some named God; I was captured.

This Spirit stayed with me at times dormant. It could not be dealt with until I stood and

CHAPTER ONE

faced the inner me looking back at me. Once again, my voice was released. I allowed some people to almost cost me the most important person to me. Thank You, Lord, for YOUR Love, Longsuffering, Mercy, and Grace.

Taking your voice is not always literal. Your "voice" maybe your health, finances, heart (emotions), spirit. Whatever "your voice" is, Never give it to anyone outside of God Himself. I would suggest you take on this mindset and disposition: I am no longer fearful, shell shocked, no longer intimidated in Jesus' name!

Lord, I speak with authority in Your name Jesus as Your mouthpiece in the earth. Remembering at times, you will need to make this very declaration to your inner man, as well.

THE INNER ME

> I am convinced and confident of this very thing, that He who has begun a good work in you will [continue to] perfect and complete it until the day of Christ Jesus [the time of His return].
> Philippians 1:6 (AMP)

CHAPTER 2
WHEN WILL YOU LEARN?

It took some time for me to learn from past mistakes. Thankfully, I have gotten better. The lessons are recognized and corrected, tweaked, or avoided quicker. Being aware of that, reflecting to avoid a retake can be extremely useful. Many adults would say, "when will you learn 'xyz'." Some knew better but rebelled, forgot, or simply ignored the signs. Whichever the operative words here are, "you learn."

THE INNER ME

The day my divorce was final, I'd been walking the track, went home, took a nap, saw this man in my dreams, and a Prophet speaking to me with instructions. I woke up, drove to Winn Dixie, and this Prophet I saw in my dreams, met me in the store. She walked up to me and my dream began to play out.

She said, "No, he is not married, and he is the one."

Then this man behind the deli counter turned around and said, "Will you marry me?"

I almost fell on the floor. My back was turned towards the Prophet. I never saw his face but heard his voice saying those same words in my dream. I turned around and my heart jumped.

He said, "I'm going to choir rehearsal now but give me a call. We can talk afterward."

The afterward turned into six years.

He loved God. We complemented each other like hands-n-gloves. He thought a thing, and before he could get home, the project was in motion. He had been the Director for the Gospel Music Workshop of America. He wanted to do a specialized training back in Dallas/Ft. Worth. Now keep in mind one thing, no excuses. I had always been married and saved; this single and saved was hard. With that, we were having sex, and I was feeling guilty every time.

CHAPTER TWO

This is where Elder Lester comes in. Whenever we did, she would call, "Was it good for you cause, it wasn't for me gal!" All the wrestling, I could not sleep." She would say, "You better be glad it was me and not Mama Jones or Bishop." JESUS help me! I am preaching, teaching, casting out demons all the while committing fornication. I tried justifying it because I was only with one person and I was trying to stop.

The Devil be damned. Sin is Sin! I would wrestle with God about it so many times. It was hard to believe God still used me. Why? I had always heard and it was drilled into us, "God can't work through unclean hands." The thing is, God would always say the same. "Your lifestyle now has nothing to do with the call and assignment on your life. Deal with it!"

During services, on some Sundays, Wednesdays, and Fridays. Elder Lester and I both would be sitting and praying that Holy Spirit did not expose me. Bishop would be preaching about this little "birdy" that freaking bird had told him dates, locations, and times about me. OMG! I felt I was the only one at times sitting in the church. It may sound funny, but trust me, I was scared to death.

Now the foolish part was, I was not scared so much about God knowing (and I was), but that Bishop would find out. He was my dad in so many ways and I never wanted to hurt him or embarrass him, his name or the church. People always associated me with him and

THE INNER ME

the church. Ironically, even when I was wrong people would excuse me because they knew I was under good, solid teaching. They would say, "You must have had a bad day, or you're not feeling well, or someone must have pushed you to your breaking point." And in fact, those were the reasons in most cases. But not for the sex that was my flesh dominating me, and not fighting effectively to use my authority to stop it.

Train up a child in the way he should go [teaching him to seek God's wisdom and will for his abilities and talents], Even when he is old, he will not depart from it.
Proverbs 22:6 (AMP)

Bishop did not condone my wrongdoing. What he did was put out an "APB" on me because he could see on his office camera when I left church.

I would ignore their saying, "Bishop wants to see you Missionary Thompson."

One day, I could not run. He came out and I almost passed out. And being the earthly Father he is to this day, he said,

"Daughter, it is okay.

You are further out than you are in. No one needs to rebuke you. You've beaten yourself up enough. Bishop loves you."
He turned and walked away. I felt like a little

CHAPTER TWO

girl when my dad would just look at me. I knew I'd disappointed him and hated myself for it. Okay, some are saying he's a man like any other man. Yes, but no he's not.

I have never known any man including my daddy like Apostle A.T. Jones, Sr. He is not perfect. He is the closest I have seen in the natural. To this day, when I go to do something, I can hear his voice. So, I have taken that to be the voice Holy Spirit uses to steer me in the path He says I should go. Remember I was raised in the church (brick-n-mortar) some were full of God, some were not.

On the other hand, the "church" still was emptying my flesh to take full control. Plainly stated, transitioning me into maturity. My inner me was getting ready to overshadow me.

THE INNER ME

> "Arise" [from spiritual depression to a new life], shine [be radiant with the glory and brilliance of the Lord]; for your light has come, And the glory and brilliance of the Lord has risen upon you. Isaiah 60:1 (AMP)

CHAPTER 3
TRIALS BEGINNING TO PAY OFF

When you become one with yourself and love you, then your trials begin to yield a harvest. Your harvest comes in several ways. They come through people, places, and things. Language Arts paid off, lol. As you read this chapter, I want you to grab a hold of these truths. Realizing that you have been bought with a high price. A price that only Jesus could pay, and you and I are recipients of that price. You and I are valuable.

THE INNER ME

Now believe it and walk in it.

Recently, one manifested itself. This past week I have been blessed to have had the first hometown book signing of my first book "And Now I Live" at The Cookbook Restaurant 7/13/19. It was such a blessing and a humbling experience. The people came out and showed love. But two things occurred during that time. I had to pick my mom up, and one of the residents was outside. Holy Spirit had me ask, "what are you doing? She responded, "I'm getting ready to order some dinner." So, I told her to get in the car, and it is on me.

Without any hesitation, she came. Well, during my presenting the book, I glanced at her crying. Holy Spirit instructed me not to look at her anymore. Then a young man came to order food, saw the book, purchased it, then walked out. Neither of these encounters had been planned or expected.

After the event, the young lady approached me and fell into my arms. She was repeatedly being told she was just crazy and imagined those things took place all through her life. Over time she began to believe she was mad as well. Words hold life and death. Please remember that. She was crying and thanking me for the transparency. The book was a portrayal of her life, her pain, her fears, and now her deliverance. What transpired was not Nathalie, but Holy Spirit.

CHAPTER THREE

Then immediately, I gave praise to God, and thanked her for coming. A door was now opened for me to go into her sphere of influence to share. We never know how, when, or where The Lord will use us for His glory.

This season has forced me to go, do, and say, "Open your mouth and do not be afraid." Many have turned against me and walked away. At those times, I had a choice. A choice to compromise my call/mantle or continue in my assignment. The assignment typically isn't lovely and sweet, yet our assignment, nonetheless. There are times we won't have time for self-preparation. Our training, for most cases, will be when we are thrust into a situation without warning. During those times, our practice should kick in.

Those lost nights of sleep, tears, ridicule, rejection, accomplishments, studying, etc... Our mentors are good or bad; the lessons will come to life. Embracing your assignments should always be looked at as a privilege to do His will in the earth, (*Thy will be done in earth, as in heaven Matthew 6:10 KJV*). When you have set yourself aside to hear the voice of God, and seeing through the eyes of God, clarity and conciseness are achieved.

There will be times that you will look back over your life and be grateful that you weren't accepted; rejoicing that you weren't invited. Celebrate the betrayal. Shout that they abandoned you. Be humbled that the

THE INNER ME

Father counted you worthy through it all! #thankfulfortherejection #itwasworthit FORWARD MOVING.

Looking inside of you, or looking back at you throughout this process can be painful. It can be outright embarrassing. Especially seeing the person you thought you were—to find out that was not who He said you are. The accomplishments or failures were never a part of the destiny set aside for you. To realize that a number of the paths you've walked were of your own making, not HIS. Yet, mercy suited your case.

> *"The accomplishments or failures were never a part of the destiny set aside for you."*

When you see within yourself, you see truth. Death was never your portion. Where you were served up like Job? For The Father has need of you. And you scream, "OK, I GIVE UP!" What more can you want from me? This life has cost me so much; God, can I PLEASE rest awhile in peace—then silence. Then you hear, "NO." So, you as Job; get up, wash your face, and FORWARD MOVE. It feels like a "Jesus moment" in the garden before His crucifixion. My Lord, this is the path You set for my life, and there is nothing I can successfully do about it but yield.

"Why?" You might ask. It's because I made a vow to Him. So, that day, through His vessels, the coals were placed upon my lips (Missionary

CHAPTER THREE

Sharon Jones at the time). Hands put to my ears by (Missionary Jessie Mae Lester), eyes and feet (Missionary Essie Mae Jones), and I said, "YES." Yes, I would give up EVERYTHING to follow YOU. Yes, I will endure hardness as a good soldier. Yes, I will go, do, and say whatever You have me to say.

A "yes" may require EVERYTHING to be mindful of your vow unto God. When you find yourself amid chaos, don't be so quick to blame the enemy. For the inner me may be the culprit. Or perhaps you are being placed in the fire for Him to show Himself strong in you.

It seems to find you no matter where you go, what you say or what you do. "IT" finds you. Then you realize some is at the hand of Daddy, while some from my doing. That part is when you want to deflect off onto something, someone, or somewhere else. The more you try—all you see is you looking back at you. Ain't that a blip, lol.

So now you regain your composure just to turn, and experience another blow. I'm honest about all the mess, and I get the short end. You know that this person is lying on me. Yet it was your mouth, and you know it. It was that nasty look you threw off, or this one: That sarcastic tone you give when you don't want to hear what someone is trying to tell you. The funny part, this is one time they are wrong. So, you suck it up and take it. You make sure your thoughts are clean. Not for your sake, but

THE INNER ME

their sake.

On the left hand [and to the north] where He works [I seek Him], but I cannot behold Him; He turns Himself to the right hand [and to the south], but I cannot see Him. But He knows the way that I take [He has concern for it, appreciates, and pays attention to it]. When He has tried me, I shall come forth as refined gold [pure and luminous]. My foot has held fast to His steps; His ways have I kept and not turned aside. Job 23:9-11 (AMPC)

Okay, you may say, "this isn't making a lick of sense, so here we go." Buckle up! Remember, Elder Lester checked me. She was raw and uncut with me. I so appreciated and respected her for that; some people know how to walk with you. They know the tone to take with you, and how to call you in. Well, this is one reason why.

My husband and I (at the time) had been going through things. I had a mother-in-law from Hell, and he was an undercover crack addict. The sad part, I didn't know he was for at least a year. He was tall, thick, bow-legged, red, and built (cut, ripped). And I loved the ground he walked on (my little god) being honest. He was getting high, but was also active in church, attentive, providing, and the sex was fabulous.

He loved both of my children and me, so you'd never know. He and my son were like twins, and that girl of mine he adored (not his

CHAPTER THREE

biological children). Through everything, he never wanted the children to be hurt. He would cry at times about our son because he knew he watched and followed him so closely.

One thing I will say, he never wanted our son to fall into that trap. He spent hours with the boys talking about life and Jesus. He would teach Balaam, Tony, and Terry (our Godsons) hard work principles and practices. Starting at sunrise, he would say, "GET UP!" He would them working on the machines, cleaning yards, building furniture...anything. OMG, he'd take them to work with him. Be it a room, or a house remodel—to a landscaping project they learned how to work HARD! They would come home late tired but loved payday.

Those moments of reflection. He worked out all the time and was a coach at one of the middle schools and in the military. We had a real-life, Lazarus experience, Lord, I can't let his C.O. know about this. This man died on me one Sunday morning in my car. He'd been off on one of his week long crack cocaine binges.

I prayed, "Lord, have him call."

He did, and I hung the phone up.

"Jesus, I'm sorry, please have him call back." and he did. I went and picked him up.

He said, "I heard your voice when you came looking for me, but I couldn't stop even though

THE INNER ME

I wanted to. I knew you could feel me in that house when you screamed,

'Jesus free, my husband!'

Then you left. This morning I heard you calling for me while you were praying, and I was able to leave the house and get to a phone."

I called my spiritual Dad, Bishop A.T. Jones, Sr. and Pastor Sharon answered the phone as if she was wide awake. Now, this is around 5:00 AM.

She said, "Bishop said, 'Bring him here.'"

It was as if they already knew. I drove to the house.

He said, "Come in the house, daughter, " and instructed Pastor Sharon to take me into the den off from the kitchen.

Then I heard him say, "Richard, come here." This man sat up, walked into their house, laid on the sofa, and was gone again. Bishop prayed over him until around 9:30 AM. How do I remember the time? Because I looked at the clock. He sat up, simultaneously at the same time his Uncle Major transitioned from TB in Eartha White Nursing Home. A modern-day miracle before my eyes, and that wasn't the first one.

That was the beginning of me being called

CHAPTER THREE

a witch, go figure. My response at that time was, "If calling on Jesus makes me a witch, so be it." I had some of my family, and even some of his family saying I was a part of a cult. Saying, "Them people over at that church have brainwashed you"—all kind of foolishness.

Nearing the end, my mother-in-law called me over to talk to me—the meeting I never saw coming. We talked about me trying to warn her of her son's addiction and her never wanting to listen or believe me. Seeing that I wasn't just the girlfriend and how she saw that I was never trying to take him away from her—but just be a daughter to her. By the time we finished talking, we had prayed and laughed. Unbeknown to me, that would be the last time I would see her before she died. Well, after 12 years, it came to an end. (I fill in the 12 years in my third book.) I didn't know, Holy Spirit was preparing me for the lane I would walk in. I call it affectionately APCOGIC Bootcamp, yes Indeed. I was being trained for warfare in the spirit, fasting, praying, standing. All of these are a part of the ministry to this day.

THE INNER ME

> The steps of a [good and righteous] man are directed and established by the LORD,
> And He delights in his way [and blesses his path]. Psalms 37:23 (AMP)

CHAPTER 4
WHEN HOLY SPIRIT MINISTERS TO YOU

As we learn and grow, we see the hand of God in action. Through this chapter, I saw how during certain months and seasons—seed time, harvest or both took place. Easton's Bible Dictionary defines God's Sovereignty as His "absolute right to do all things according to His own good pleasure." That's nothing special to most. Yet, it should be. It can prevent mishaps as well as position you for the greater.

THE INNER ME

2 April 2019 9:00 AM - 12:00 PM call and Holy Spirit ministers to your inner man.

Just as I have had "Many Novembers" Holy Spirit just reminded me "Nathalie, you've had many months of March as well." While sitting here on our (JMT) John Maxwell Team, with (Mark Cole Mentorship Tribe 9:00 AM call), I was reminded it was:

- March 9, 2005, released after heart issues from Bank of America five years.

- March 9, 2009, LifesReDesign Ministry Intl, Inc. Launched from typing the vision, starting at 8:00 AM - 11:00 PM NONSTOP.

- March 13, Birthday of Grandmother and twin cousins, transitioning of Father and Aunt/Mother Bernice who helped raise me.

- March 24-26 I had three heart attacks back to back.

- March 24 week 2017 in Baptist Hospital one week from a stroke on right side. Living in a real-life Hell on earth, they find it amusing.

- March 8-12 2019 JMT IMC after 20 years studying, teaching, and applying.

- March 25, 2019 in Baptist Hospital from stroke, speech, walking and balance affected. At IMC prior to walking in "stroke zone."

CHAPTER FOUR

- March 2020 my OFFICIAL Global Launch of the Apostolic Covering, ARISE Global Alliance in remembrance of my Spiritual Midwives (Apostles).

The late Elder Jessie Mae Lester (ARISE Fellowship Intl) and Elder Essie Mae Jones (Reflections radio broadcast and "I've Got the Key Outreach Ministry"). Both labored with me for years until they birthed me into my purpose. Both have transitioned and left mantles and charges deposited within me to carry on. FORWARD MOVING!

Lord Help! What am I supposed to do now? You gave me my mouth to use for a living and business. I know there is a lesson here, but my brain, eyes, and heart are at a loss. There are assignments You gave me to put in place. Now I'm not mobile, really God?

You find yourself reflecting over your life accomplishments and failures as if it's been a total waste of time. Whatever all the Hell you've gone through, and for what? You mean I could've done "such-n-such" and never dealt with... Oh yeah, you go through those moments. I would beat myself up because I did. Then I remembered this one crucial truth.

> I assure you and most solemnly say to you, a slave is not greater than his master, nor is one who is sent greater than the one who sent him.
> John 13:16 (AMP)

THE INNER ME

When you take the time to stop, look, and listen that inner you (spirit man) will speak. Jesus in the Garden of Gethsemane Mark 14:32-50 had a moment. Although Jesus never called to record, He did question God. Do I have to do this? Knowing that, although He asked, He was going to be obedient regardless. Does that take anything away from who I am because I question God? Of course not. It made me realize one truth, how dependent and in the relationship I am with the Father.
For most, that makes absolutely no sense whatsoever, lol, I know. This is how I'm wired.

Numbers and words have meanings that can make or break us. My identity was accidentally mixed up with another woman. We shared both first and last name, birthday, but the year was different by one year: words, specific times, and numbers.

My life has been one not so different than many. The difference may be that I question my life's purpose. If I'm going to do something, it has to have a meaning associated with it. Good, bad, or the indifferent, there will be. When looking at March, it is the third month. Me being a numbers person, I looked it up. I found myself in them in some fashion, regardless of the source.

"The number 3 biblically represents divine wholeness, completeness, and perfection. If there ever was a desire to highlight an idea, thought, event, or noteworthy figure in the

CHAPTER FOUR

Bible for their prominence, the number 3 was used to put a divine stamp of completion or fulfillment on the subject." Voices of Faith: Is '3' something of a holy number in Christianity? https://www.kansascity.com > living > religion > article1319649 "Biblical number 3 General meaning."

People for whom numeral 3 has a significant meaning to are great thinkers. They have a passion for learning about the truth at all costs, even if in that way, they are depriving themselves of happiness in some way. This means that you are the person, who will dedicate your life in the search for the truth. At the same time, you may never care about your own wellbeing. This could be seen as a sacrifice that Jesus did for all people." Dreamingandsleeping.com

"Bible numerology number 3 stands for the Trinity, trine and triad which are the three dimensions. Namely, Father, the Son, and the Holy Spirit or Ghost. In a broader way, the bible number 3 symbolizes growth and multiplication. There were three disciples of God—Peter, John and James—who accompanied Jesus Christ to the garden of Gethsemane. These disciples symbolize light, love and life respectively. In the Bible, Jesus Christ asked Peter "Lovest thou me?" three times that refer to the love over three surfaces of consciousness, namely, the conscious mind, the super conscious mind and the subconscious mind. It is also avers that if all the three planes

of consciousness agrees to club together, the power of Christ will prevail. The bible number 3 is very vital in the story of Jesus Christ or one can say His story is a story of number 3. Jesus was denied by Peter thrice and after three days he rose. He was crucified in between two thieves that symbolize the divine system of faith and belief. Twelve is the higher vibration of the number three and Jesus sat with twelve of his disciples. Also the Judas haggled for thirty silver pieces which is again a vibration of bible number three.

Jesus Christ raised three folks from the clutches of death. There were three major feasts in the Bible- Tabernacle, Weeks and the unleavened bread. There were three gifts of the grace and also Jonah dwelled for three days inside a whale. According to the Old testaments bible number three symbolizes the First Trinity that is Adam, Eve and the Child. It signifies expansion and expression. The other trinities surviving in this world are body, spirit and soul and the three divisions of consciousness of the mind- conscious, super conscious and subconscious about which we have already mentioned in the new testaments. http://www.astrovera.com/bible-religion/168-bible-number-3.html"

Trust me. I could have kept going on because while researching this, it was good eating to my spirit. Now, I shared this because at times we feel so insignificant. But through the eyes of our Creator, we are masterpieces, with flaws

CHAPTER FOUR

and all. Looking at yourself, owning who you are will be challenging, but equally rewarding. The freedom that accompanies you becoming one with your inner man; I can't put into words.

THE INNER ME

> O LORD, you have searched me [thoroughly] and have known me. You know when I sit down and when I rise up [my entire life, everything I do];
> You understand my thought from afar. You scrutinize my path and my lying down, And You are intimately acquainted with all my ways. Even before there is a word on my tongue [still unspoken], Behold, O LORD, You know it all. You have enclosed me behind and before, And [You have] placed Your hand upon me.
> Psalm 139:1-5 (AMP)

CHAPTER 5
TRUSTING IN YOUR "WHY" TRADE OFF

You can't start a new chapter until you've completed the current face-2-face. How can you move forward when forward looks like an impossible dream? The people you've always trusted you now realize the page has turned. Not that they're bad people. Their time of connection has come to an end. An end that you thought could or would never happen.

THE INNER ME
Affirmation for Accomplishments

- I Shall Live and Not Die and Declare the works of the Lord
- Security for significance
- Significance makes a difference
- Financial gain for future potential
- Hard pill to swallow but realize it's necessary
- Scarcity for His abundance
- HE shall supply all my need and grant my desires
- Immediate pleasure for personal growth
- No
- Exploration for focus
- Focus
- Quantity of life for Quality of life
- Quality for Quantity will fade
- Acceptable for excellence
- Excellence as unto the Lord
- Addition for multiplication
- Never despise the day of small beginnings
- 1st half for 2nd half
- Reflections

You find yourself getting ready to call when a problem, a funny moment, a success has occurred. Then you hear Holy Spirit say, "NO! That season has passed." "Why?", You ask. "Where I'm taking you, the things I have planned for you. You can't be limited or bound. I've allowed you to feel abandoned, rejected, loved, ill, triumphant, and sometimes all in one day. It has been strategic with purpose." "I, GOD, never execute idle tasks or assignments,

CHAPTER FIVE

and neither will you... FORWARD MOVING."

My, I AM...
- Fearfully and wonderfully made in His image
- The redeemed from the hand of the enemy
- The head and not the tail
- Above and never beneath
- Full of joy, peace, and love
- Forgiven, delivered and made free by Jesus
- Strong in the Lord and in the power of His might
- An overcomer and conqueror
- The lender and not a borrower
- Abraham's heir to the blessing
- A giver and supporter of the lost
- A light in darkness
- A repairer of the breach
- Called to establish God's Word here in the earth realm
- Called to the lost and rejected to revive
- A beacon set up on a hill
- Being used of the Lord to do great things in the earth
- Divinely connected to those that will sow increase into the vision which Holy Spirit has placed within me
- I do not fret or have anxiety about anything
- A child of the Most High God with nothing lacking, broken or missing in my life or those in covenant agreement with me in Yeshua's name

It seems natural to trust God and thrive when all is bright lights and glitter. You will pay your tithes, pray, fast, give, witness every

THE INNER ME

free moment you get. God's hand is upon you for good. I am blessed abundantly. There is nothing broken, lacking or missing in my life. I am the lender, and I don't have to borrow... Yes, shouting out declarations of wealth, physical and mental, and spiritual.

During a rough patch, reality said, "Who are you?" Then challenged me to stand upon who Nathalie said she is, NOT who Nathalie was. There is a difference. For "is" represents the present time, "was" represents the past. When you have a face-2-face encounter (the inner me looking back at me), you will never be "past tense" again. If you do, you will die. So, you must gather, decree and declare your "I AM" declarations over yourself.

This doesn't require the Prophet to come and speak to you. You become your own prophetic voice and speak the Word (not emotions) of God over you. Cover yourself, your family, your home, and those connected to you. Believe it, there will be times, you can't find another voice. In those times, you must become the voice of God in your own life. You can do this as you begin to become acquainted with your inner man. For The Father desires a relationship with His Spirit within you. That is why He gave us Jesus to reconcile us back to Him.

CHAPTER FIVE

"For The Good Of Them"
Rev. Milton Brunson and the Thompson Community Singers (1988)

The race is not given, to the swift nor to the strong,
But to the one that endures, until the end,
They'll be problems,
And sometimes you walk alone, but I know,
that I know that I know,
It will work out, yes it will for the good of them...who loves the Lord.

Eyes have not seen, and neither have ears heard,
The things that God has prepared for them...

Sometimes, you may have to cry,
And sometimes, you may have to may have to moan
But I know, that I know, that I know,
Things will work out, yes they will,
For the good of them...who love the Lord.

No matter what the problem,
You can't solve them,
They will come, but don't, you worry.
It will work out, for the good of them who, loves the Lord.

THE INNER ME

> Now the Lord is the Spirit, and where the Spirit of the Lord is, there is liberty [emancipation from bondage, true freedom].
> 2 Corinthians 3:17 (AMP)

CHAPTER 6
SOME THINGS YOU SHOULDN'T FORGET
24 JULY 2019

While talking to my mother today, a memory I'd completely forgotten rushed in. We would go to a house prayer service with a Pastor by the name of Mother Wright. She would pray and flow in the prophetic with such precision. It would amaze me back then. Until later, I realized she too, was a part of my process for who God called me to be today.

THE INNER ME

I remember one day, I was driving across the Matthews Bridge. Suddenly, my car door flew open. Others were in the car to bear witness. ALL the doors were closed and locked. When I got home, my mom told me to call Mother Wright she'd called. When I spoke to her, she told me to come to her house. When I arrived, she said, "Sit down." Then she began to pray. She began to tell me what had happened earlier and several other things that had been occurring for about two weeks to me. After the word was released, she told me where it had come from. She'd had a visitor before that was sent to her. The funny part is, the person that referred her thought she was a witch. Why? It's because that person was ignorant of the prophetic and praying in your heavenly language.

Nevertheless, the person came and explained that she and her husband were separated, and he was having an affair with a younger woman. She went on to say that she wanted her out of the picture. Well, at first thought, okay we will pray a prayer of agreement for your marriage to be restored, that's acceptable. But that wasn't what she meant by wanting her out of the picture. She wanted her dead. Without saying, she refused and told her to leave her house.

Now I told this because I was the other woman, 17 years old at the time. Before you condemn me to Hell, in my first book, "And Now I Live," it's stated I was not aware of him

CHAPTER SIX

being married when we met. In fact, she had moved out of the house and all. By the time I became aware of her, I was pregnant with our son.

Unfortunately, she got worse after our son was born. She had tried to speak word curses of sickness and death over him. But every time she did, something happened to her son. It sounds like a Moses, Miriam, and Aaron situation to me. Now, this is when the Word of God becomes life lived off the pages to you.

Do not touch My anointed ones! Do no harm to My prophets! Psalms 105:15 (NIV)

Don't delude yourselves: no one makes a fool of God! A person reaps what he sows. Galatians 6:7 (CJB)

Moreover, I tell you this: on the Day of Judgement people will have to give account for every careless word they have spoken; for by your own words you will be acquitted, and by your own words you will be condemned." Matthew 12:36-37 (CJB)
The Word of God will always remain true.

I was on the receiving end as well. For no matter how you slice it, I was wrong. I was sleeping with the music director. We will call him as well as my children's dad. Young or older, I knew sex outside of marriage is wrong. We try and excuse our wrongs without any merit. Later, I was challenged and checked on

THE INNER ME

one part of that. It was interesting how the outcome came. God cannot lie. We will reap a harvest of whatever we have sown.

Some right now are preparing their harvest by ignorantly operating in witchcraft, following dark magic, practicing voodoo, entertaining familiar spirits, and so much more. When someone tries to give you instruction or correct you, then you rebel. All the while, the voice within is telling you to listen, be quiet, get out of your feelings. Doesn't that sound familiar? Don't act like you don't understand. Don't act like you don't hear them talking. Now, even more profound, you listen to me speaking to you through them. If you continue, I will bring you to utter shame. Your measure of grace is running short. Pride comes before a fall.

Now, when Holy Spirit begins to speak, and we still ignore His voice, we are on a slow, slippery slope to a reprobated mind or death—be it spiritual or natural. How can I reference all of these? At one time or another, it has happened to me. My inner self was looking, screaming back at me. Or someone that I knew out of love and obedience to God was coming as a warning. Dark works were never my thing even with that, does that make my sin any less than other? No. Being stubborn and rebellious is as witchcraft.

Some have fallen into works of dark magic because of being broken. Life has beaten them down for so long until facing themselves is

CHAPTER SIX

terrifying. The people they interact with cross them, family bash them, and business or ministry sucks. What happens when you don't have that mentor that knows the way to guide you? Where are the children of God that are to pull you up without wounding you? And most of all, where are those intercessors that said we're praying for you?

Well, at some point, we know we will be tested and tried. But hold fast for we shall come forth as pure gold from the fire—beaten, broken, and purified.

THE INNER ME

> As for you, what you intended against me for evil, God intended for good, in order to accomplish a day like this-to preserve the lives of many people. Genesis 50:20 (BSB)

CHAPTER 7
LOOKING WITHIN

Williamsburg, VA 31 July 2019—My Lord, did He take me through a refresher course. It was much needed. "Nathalie, be honest with yourself. Some things you know what you know. Some things you can't ignore anymore. Some things you have no need to seek clarity. Some things you take the initiative to prune and cut off from the root (deep). I've given you the tools to do. I AM the Lord, I AM Sovereign. I'm not coming off My throne, nor sending aid."

THE INNER ME

Stop looking to others for what God created within you. The mere fact that when you get a thought, a vision clearly is seen through your mind's eye, should be a clue. A clue that it was given to you not to the person(s) you are now consulting if it is for you. At some point in time, we've all been in that place. But with that also comes a time of growth and maturity; a time you get off of milk and eat meat. Think about this. You may be one that will take "me" out and place yourself.

"I decree and declare. Having been subjected to always second-guessing the voice of God (Holy Spirit) speaking to me and having broken away from such bondage and manipulation... I shall NEVER again allow myself to be entangled in Jesus' name. There is nothing lacking, broken, or missing within me.

I have each day ALL provisions to create, obtain and be a blessing in Jesus' name. I am the lender, not the borrower. I am above, not beneath—the head, and not the tail. My words birth life and multiplication for supernatural increase in wealth, health, physical and spiritual things in Jesus' name.

All who are in covenant agreement with me will receive from the oil that overflows from my cup in Jesus' name. My life is valuable in the earth. It is used as a blueprint for others to become overcomers in Jesus' name. For that too, was a teaching moment for me to grow from. It is now my obligation to pass that knowledge onto

CHAPTER SEVEN

others that will come after me. Be it unto me In Jesus' name, AMEN."

They will never [on any account] follow a stranger but will run away from him because they do not know the voice of strangers or recognize their call. John 10:5 (AMPC)

DID YOU DO IT?

Are you able to face yourself when you are the one who has administered the pain? Are you true to yourself to own up to the consequences of the day? The inner me "you" will speak, scream, laugh, and rejoice, and will not yet be seen. Is it possible that you, from a child, were taught that you're not to express emotions? By showing emotions, you show weakness.

When I am asked to conduct masterminds for groups or organizations, they don't realize what they're walking into. Over those 5-8 weeks overall, there is a big-screen displaying our lives. Therefore, the entire group can see, judge, and learn about each other. It's yet another way the inner you looks back at you. You may be reluctant to share in the beginning. However, as time moves forward, you see that the inner me has more in common, more to learn, more to give, and more gain. The process is needful to strive. It is needed to soar, to create, to duplicate, and to impart.

There will be times that you will look back over your life and will be grateful that you

THE INNER ME

weren't accepted. You will rejoice that you weren't invited. You will celebrate the betrayal, and shout that they abandoned you. May you then be humbled that The Father counted you worthy through it all! #thankfulfortherejection #itwasworthit FORWARD MOVING

When your mind and your spirit are at peace, your thoughts and actions are free to be healthy, free to be focused, and free to be productive.

> *"You cannot force others to be truly peaceful."*

You cannot force others to be truly peaceful. You cannot shame them into it. Yet, by your example, you can draw them into the power of your own peacefulness. You must DO YOUR PART! Holy Spirit is NOT a waiter or genie in a bottle. Faith WITHOUT works is dead! Never allow the opinions and definitions of others (regarding you) to poison who YOU are. Sometimes they are merely regretting their decisions for their life. Continue to love and pray for them unless Holy Spirit instructs you to stop, then stop.

Carry on with your day. The phrase "six of one a half a dozen of the other," simply put. There are those that no matter what, you can't please or change. That was a lesson that took me years to learn and apply. After beating yourself up, and second-guessing, "Did I or didn't I do it?" You sometimes forget if you did or didn't. People's words start to take root within, and you become who or what

CHAPTER SEVEN

they say you are. Did you do it? Have you lost your identity? If so, take it back, and become the absolute best version of you. You are fearfully and wonderfully made in His image and likeness. Then you shall with confidence answer, "Yes, I did do it!" Let them ponder how, when, and where.

THE INNER ME

> Study and do your best to present yourself to God approved, a workman [tested by trial] who has no reason to be ashamed, accurately handling and skillfully teaching the word of truth.
> 2 Timothy 2:15 (AMP)

CHAPTER 8
SCHEDULING GOD

There are so many who have lost their "childlike" faith. When we first began, we spent every free moment with God hungry to be in His presence. Now our lives are "busy," so we schedule in a time to commune with God. Some say 3AM, 5AM, 9PM, 12AM is their 1-on-1 with God. If we've dedicated a set time with Him, how does He fit in with the remaining 23-24hrs?

THE INNER ME

"When God has CALLED YOU and HAS CHOSEN YOU to something, and has PROCESSED you through it and BIRTHED YOU in it, it's hard to pull away from it! It becomes part of your very makeup. It is engrafted in your DNA and every fiber of your being. It becomes not only your lifestyle, but your life!" #CalledToPrayer #iPray #iGovern #iLegislate #iSee #iHear #iProphesy"

—Apostle Irish Jackson
Founder of Awakening Global Intercessors

Let us reflect on the introduction of the book: This is just a glimpse of what did (and still is) taking place even today. Let me give you a couple of examples that created this false world for themselves only to suffer at the very creation they formed—All because they didn't follow the blueprint The Word of God. You know that saying, "when you know better you do better."

    Eli and his sex-addicted sons, Hophni and Phinehas, because he chose to ignore their behavior knowing how they defiled the Temple of God with their orgies, rapes, and anything else they desired. Although he loved God, his failure to protect that which was placed in his charge (the Ark of the Covenant) cost him his life. Eli fell back, broke his neck, and died, after hearing the ark was taken.
Then there is David, (whom God loved). His sex addiction cost him his son. He was plotting and scheming all the while serving God. Yet people say there is no way you can truly

CHAPTER EIGHT

love God, be saved, and sin. WRONG! It took his Prophet assigned to David to show him, himself.

Have mercy upon me, O God, according to Your steadfast love; according to the multitude of Your tender mercy and loving-kindness blot out my transgressions. Wash me thoroughly [and repeatedly] from my iniquity and guilt and cleanse me and make me wholly pure from my sin! For I am conscious of my transgressions and I acknowledge them; my sin is ever before me. Against You, You only, have I sinned and done that which is evil in Your sight, so that you are justified in Your sentence and faultless in Your judgment. Behold, I was brought forth in [a state of] iniquity; my mother was sinful who conceived me [and I too am sinful]. Behold, You desire truth in the inner being; make me, therefore, to know wisdom in my inmost heart. Purify me with hyssop, and I shall be clean [ceremonially]; wash me, and I shall [in reality] be whiter than snow. Make me to hear joy and gladness and be satisfied; let the bones which You have broken rejoice. Hide Your face from my sins and blot out all my guilt and iniquities. Create in me a clean heart, O God, and renew a right, persevering, and steadfast spirit within me. Cast me not away from Your presence and take not Your Holy Spirit from me. Restore to me the joy of Your salvation and uphold me with a willing spirit. Then will I teach transgressors Your ways, and sinners shall be converted and return to You. Psalm 51:1-13 (AMPC)

THE INNER ME

[For that matter], why do I live [dangerously as I do, running such risks that I am] in peril every hour? [I assure you] by the pride which I have in you in [your [a]fellowship and union with] Christ Jesus our Lord, that I die daily [I face death every day and die to self].
1 Corinthians 15:30-32 (AMP)

Each of these reference points show that the person was aware of their actions yet wouldn't resist the temptation of carrying them through. That has been me a time or two or three or more. But the grace of God has kept me from my inner me. I referenced "sex" because that was my drug of choice. You can plug in whatever yours was or still is. When I would be planning some of the things, I could hear my inner me talking back at me.

Believe me, I reaped several times. It finally became apparent that my granddaughter was a crucial component in teaching me a lesson. For some of you, this is going to sound crazy. For others, it will begin to shed light on many occurrences in your life. I would find myself in positions that were of my own doing because "I loved" that man.

Unfortunately, it would be at the expense of her. This was an innocent angel whom I love with all my heart. Holy Spirit asked,

"Do you really?

Well, if you do, why keep placing her in harm's

CHAPTER EIGHT

way?

Why don't you do the right thing?"

It came at the price of walking away from someone that had we never slept together, my life would be so different now. We were in sync. Ministry flowed through us like hands-n-gloves. Lesson learned: Denying your flesh isn't just about sex. Our "it", whatever it is, covers a wide range. It sets a domino effect into play. Just like Eli, it could've cost her life and mine as well. Like David, it was being covered up at the expense of someone else. The list can go on and on, just think about it. That inner me looking back at me is crucial to our success or demise.

THE INNER ME

> The day that you hear my voice, harden not your hearts as you did in the rebellion
> Deuteronomy 1:26-38 Psalm 95:6-11
> Hebrews 3:7-19

CHAPTER 9
SOUNDPROOFING

My Lord girl, can you hear yourself? You need to take your own medicine. And that I did. I prayed the same prayer—but this time something was different. Nathalie was required to shut out every distraction, including myself (my thoughts). Okay, God, it's all in or none! I'm very much aware when I hear your voice I am trying to speak my thoughts over you. So many opportunities have passed by.

THE INNER ME

So many open doors that I've allowed to be shut listening to the "opinions" of others.

Father, please forgive me for not obeying Your Instructions. Thank You, Father, for being merciful and patient with me. I stand before You God under an open Heaven with outstretched hands in total surrender to You. Empty me, Father, of everything that displeases You. Empty me, cut away everything, every person, every place that has or will cause me to stumble or even fall. I give it all to You in Jesus' name, Amen.

Every so often, there is a need to get off onto the emergency embankment and send up intentional worship and prayer—that kind when you hear nothing that's going on or see anything. A posture of prayer that drains everything out of you, yet fills you to overflowing. That place when even you feel that He is not listening, but you're going in and being like Jacob. You are willing to wrestle with the Angel and say, "I'm not letting go until You bless me." Well, in fact, it says it was God Himself.

Those times where you will go so deep, you can feel the earth move. All your senses are on high alert, and you are locked and loaded. Soundproof the atmosphere. It needs to be clear to everyone, that this is not the time for them to say or do anything that would break that connection. Even typing this I've had to clap my hands and stomp my feet a few times.

CHAPTER NINE

As simple as this is, it's so hard for people to do.

Namaste (Hindu greeting) for Americans it's done in the manner of us putting our hands together for prayer.

The soundproof room: Are you saying that God is not speaking? Or are you just not listening to the soundproof room? The vibration will either let God in or will keep him out of the soundproof room, Your "inner me" I had a meeting with my local covering Apostle and Prophet last night. All I can say: when Holy Spirit directs you to go submit and connect, obey and go! Organizational instructions and clarity are in place and in agreement. It was the most relaxed meeting I've ever had. The Father is Pleased.

Although I am older than both of them holds no weight. Both of them operate with such governmental authority in Kingdom (not dogmatic or manipulative). Upon meeting them (physically, mentally, emotionally, and spiritually), the ministry, family, everything required a TOTAL makeover. The Father sent me into my Psalm 91 place at Harvest, and I allowed Him to place me back onto the Potter's wheel. Still standing on the words spoken to me from our first meeting three years ago. "You've been in bondage for so long, that you don't know when you're FREE." Well, freedom looks and feels good from the inside out.

THE INNER ME

Yes, I stay very close to that soundproof place. It has become a very peaceful place. Even when what is received isn't always comfortable, but it is necessary. There is a soundproof room within a room. Never be rude or disrespectful. It's a learned behavior. You can be fully engaged in conversation yet, still in the soundproof room. You are attentive to everyone and everything, but still able to hear clearly God's voice in the midst. I'm engaged while my hands are in a praying position. Going in while conversing, crying, laughing whatever, however. Not being invisible just within a soundproof space within a space with The Father. Man should always pray, pray without ceasing. Soundproof.

LOOKING IN THE FACE OF THE ABUSER

I remember being at the courthouse with my husband and running into one of the guys that raped me (Georgia train).

He walked up to me and said,

"Don't I know you?"

My response, "Yes, it's been a long time."

"Well, I'm down here having to take care of a case," he said.

CHAPTER NINE

Yeah, my husband and I are here regarding his son. He starts to say, "God is sho'nuff good," and my reply was, "Yes, He is."

He said, "It was good to see you." I say, "Same here."

Then I turn to Terrence and say,

"Remember when I told you about the seven guys that pulled the Georgia train on me when I was in junior high school?"

He says, "Yes." Well, he was one of them.

Then he stopped and said, "I'm glad I didn't know that beforehand."

Well, we go handle our business and come back to the café. Who walks in? He does. I said to myself, "Watch he come to our table," and he did. He asked if he could join us. I said, "Sure."

And we just began to talk about how good God has been over the years. How he'd delivered us from things and how we knew it was nobody but Him. Then he leaves. Terrence turns to me and says, "How the Hell did you let him sit here with us?" This came along with several other colorful words.

Easy, I hold no grudges. I've been delivered, healed, and freed.

THE INNER ME

Terrance says in disbelief, "There is no way in Hell I could do that.

That's something that can't be forgiven."

My response was, "That's the difference between the two of us."

When you allow God to be in control of your life, you take on Jesus' characteristics. My life lived before, and my husband must be witnessed in word and deed (action). Food for thought: To those who are married, single, with or without children. This applies to the saved and unsaved, regardless of your faith or lack thereof. Your life is on a Big Screen for someone somewhere. What life movie are we displaying?

Toxicity inside (hostility, guilt, unforgiveness) will lead you to an early grave—physically, mentally, or both. When you look at yourself in the mirror or internally, you'll never see the person you can be. The reflection will only be the person you've allowed yourself to become. This is only another point of repossessing your power. Yeah, sometimes you must reclaim your power from yourself. It's called accountability.

> And forgive us our [f]debts, as we have forgiven our debtors [letting go of both the wrong and the resentment].
> Matthew 6:12 (AMP)

CHAPTER NINE

"Safe in His Arms"
Rev. Milton Brunson and the Thompson
Community Singers (1986)

Because the Lord is my shepherd
I have everything I need
He lets me rest in the meadows grass
And He leads me besides the quiet stream
He restores my failing health
And helps me to do what honors
Him the most
That's why I'm safe
Safe in His arms
When the storm of life is raging
And the billows roll
So glad He shall hide me
Safe in His arms
So glad, He shall hide me
Safe in His arms

> Blessed [anticipating God's presence, spiritually mature] are the pure in heart [those with integrity, moral courage, and godly character], for they will see God.
> Matthew 5:8 (AMP)

CHAPTER 10
PURPOSE IN THE EARTH

Through this program, I indeed found myself face-2-face with myself. Having been or living with each of these. OpFaith, Operation Faith Transition Transportation, and Re-Development Program. Our focus is on victims of abuse (sex, child labor, etc...), the ex-offender (Veteran and non-vets, male and female), alternative lifestyle, feeding families, and those re-entering society. We also are focused on those outside, serving the same

THE INNER ME

sentence.

It is customary to disregard the husband, wife, mother, aunt, and children. Yet, they take that sentence passed down as well. Their world has been changed immediately.

Homeless veterans, abused, etc... If you want a cause that will give back, consider Operation Faith (OpFaith), a 501(c)(3). (Prisons mental or physical) Do not discriminate against age, nationality, religion, economic class, gender, or education) they have served us. Now is the time we can be servants. It is a strong belief of ours that "It takes a village to raise a family," and "what doesn't break you will make you," welcome to Our Village!

2011 OpFaith's "Wounded Soldier ARISE!" was birthed while putting together one of the fundraiser flyers for OpFaith, my heart began to sob. Going through to license the photos for us to use was grueling. Scrolling through seeing the once vibrant soldiers, both male/female alike, now broken in spirit and body. Lord, what have we as a people done? They left home to serve their country. Now some have returned and have nowhere to turn. So many mentally, physically, sexually broken, damaged, and now discarded.

Game recognize game. Those we are to appeal to want Genuine and Authentic TRUTH!

What can I do as an individual as well as the

CHAPTER TEN

ministry at large? Reflecting on Leo, my oldest brother, imagining what condition could he have been in if he had returned from Vietnam? He had been shot. The gunfire was too heavy to recover the soldiers. He laid there for four days. Was it a blessing in disguise for him not to return home? Oh God, am I wrong for even having that thought? Tears building, shortening of breath, and hands shaking even typing the words. Even more, I understand for the scriptures that LifesReDesign was birthed upon. Once again, I'm reminded The Father does know best. I've got to walk away for a minute, it's too much! All these years and I still miss him.

A lane that I've had to do for so long and would do it at a snail pace, is soliciting donations. Knowing that to continue OpFaith, we need those to aid in providing items and donations to our cause and mission. We are sending out to Duval, Broward, Vance, Bernalillo counties and various parishes in LA. With businesses, organizations, and personal donations, we will provide personal hygiene items, families with groceries, homeless with meals, socks/gloves/blankets. In some areas, we are working with those that will allow access for showers as well. Those locations will provide a change of clothing. Each donation is tax-deductible. We can do this and much more with your help."

THE INNER ME

> For I was hungry, and you gave Me something to eat; I was thirsty, and you gave Me something to drink; I was a stranger, and you invited Me in; I was naked, and you clothed Me; I was sick, and you visited Me [with help and ministering care]; I was in prison, and you came to Me [ignoring personal danger].' Then the righteous will answer Him, 'Lord, when did we see You hungry, and feed You, or thirsty, and give You something to drink? And when did we see You as a stranger, and invite You in, or naked, and clothe You? And when did we see You sick, or in prison, and come to You?' The King will answer and say to them, 'I assure you and most solemnly say to you, to the extent that you did it for one of these brothers of Mine, even the least of them, you did it for Me.
> Matthew 25:35-40 (AMP)

"We are not exempt from pain, sufferings, trials, tribulations, misfortunes, sickness Diseases, or whatever may come our way. Some folks are going to be shocked. They counted you out. They couldn't get with you. They mistreated you. Talked about you. Lied on you. Some tried to use you. Some tried to prostitute the anointing. Some told you that you didn't hear God correctly. Oh, but I want you to know we are in the Eighth Month and be the third day. God is about to call your name. The tables are turning. It's your time. New friends, new connections. Your family [is going to] be SURPRISE, SURPRISE."

—August 3, 2019, at 11:33 PM
From Apostle Patricia Harris

Journal Section

Write your thoughts & reflections